I0479609

RAINBOW GRAFFITI

A collection of poem

Dr. Bhratri Bhushan

CONTENTS

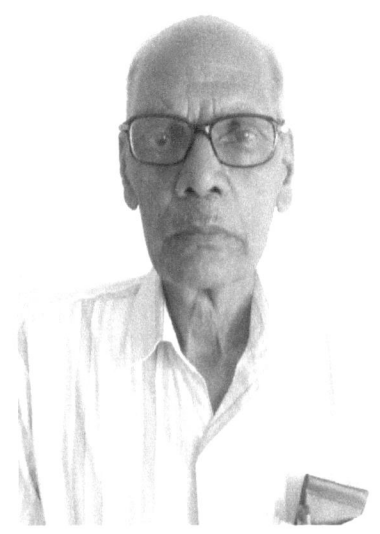

Dedicated to Sh. Rajendra Singh (Jhal)

A WEEKEND WITH MY
FRIEND WEAKENED

Pushing the earth with her two hands,
wheels turning, each turn advancing
agony to the doorstep of despair.
She keeps smiling, just a twitch;
lately her courage is hamstrung,
she must keep up appearances though.

In her dreams, she runs across town;
wondering why she isn't out of breath.
When she wakes up from such dreams,
she wonders why she is dyspneic.
For once in her not very long life,
she looks at the clock, and prays
for the night to fall.

There was a time, less than a decade ago,
when she'd look out of her car's window,
and wonder, what made the debilitated go on.
Scoffed she, at terms like "differently abled",
but now she just hates these words.
Weeks ago she told me not to sugarcoat,
because life's not been kind,
and nature sure doesn't need a cat's paw.

Everyone is dealt with a deck of cards,
rigged however, but that's all one's got.
And until your back breaks with
that one final straw, it's all a dim illusion.
She goes on to tell, what makes her go on:
her dreams and the memories,
which become brighter everyday, while
each passing moment makes the future
more bleak than before.

BARELY FUNCTIONING

In this continuum of existence,
where all is one, one is all;
I declare myself, as a bubble
of its own being.
I always make a list
and compartmentalise,
reducing people
to chequered boxes.

I argue hard and fast,
about the wave form a particle
and particle that the wave is.
Exploring the unknown,
I talk about the final frontier
and beyond.
Yet I'm scared of myself.

Talk to me about the development
of sexuality in a child,
you'll have a conversation.
And make no mistake,
I'm a reformer, teeming
with philosophy.
All empty and without a spark,
for it's me who I don't know.

DR. BHRATRI BHUSHAN

I eye the sky, but
the earth beneath my feet
doesn't belong to me.

I fight, with all my might
with this knot in my stomach;
knit whenever the flower of
my being tries to break out of
the bud, like a lotus out of the mud.
Just so I can spend another
dreamless night, and a day dreaming,
what someone else will think of me.
Instead of being who I am,
I strive to be anything but me.

Some moments of craziness
sneak up on me though;
and in those evanescent motions
of hands of time, I am alive,
energised of my shadow's embrace.
I don't surrender, quickly recover,
to being this air tight, forced upon
container of mishaps that history
has culminated in.
And then I look blankly,
a creeping listlessness ensues,
knowing fully, that all I have to do,
is to look at life in its eyes,
grab my own hand and wade,
through the uncharted waters
of my life, while I still can.

ENTROPY IN REVERSE

Each electron is a universe, each universe an electron of an atom of another universe;
siphoning portals of black holes, traversing between universes, infinite and looping.
Curves of probabilities, no pinpointed certainties, to top it all of there are quantum fluctuations,
making entire multiverses out of nothing at all, and quarks spinning, literally like bananas.

The eerie, unmistakable déjà vu of having experienced the most peculiar happenstances,
and falling in love with a stranger, like quantum entanglement of two minds surreal.
All this makes me wonder, who am I and what am I doing here. If its all an illusion then,
who says illusions are not real; to me anything and everything in any realm is as real as any other.

Sparring with the factions of my mind, and groping in the darkness imparted by shadows
of unsubstantiated dogmas, I grapple with any solace handy, committing the biggest mistake.
All I can do, must do, is to become an empty vessel, receptive of the rain of existence,
pouring around me forever. And be a witness of

what is, how it is, not asking why.
For only the witness in me is constant, in any plane
of consciousness or otherwise, and it's not me,
it's just a point of observation in the infinite awareness, no matter how many multiverses are there.

CYCLIC CIRCUSES

Twice every decade or so, circus arrives in town;
one says it's the Hail Mary, another says it's upside down.
People let themselves slip, playing right in their hands,
enmeshed swiftly in tentacles, not realising that there heroes,
are nothing but ventriloquists of what doesn't even lurk behind.

Like a shepherd, the hidden hand lures herds of people to an abattoir;
the trick greatest being the deception of its non-existence, a double negative.
Here they are today again, some faces familiar, with a make believe baggage,
while others arrive fresh, in a cacophony of deep delusion, oh-so enticing.

A chap reads the news on a smoke screen, never truly revealing the orchestra;
but only the puppets that dance to the rhythm of bubbles bursting, biting dust.
Some printed words, carefully crafted and incisive but just abrading the surface,

swirl emotions unwarranted; while the pied pipers hide their smiles,
behind thick masks of thinly veiled intentions, in plain sight of ignorance blind.

When a time comes, already too late, of someone sitting behind an oak desk,
entreating me to hold my neighbour's hand and smile without a reason;
I will still not believe, however earnest they are being. My trust so violated,
stands stranded, alone and confused, amid this crowd of shrewness embodied,
that I don't know, if I can trust myself, let alone those who manipulate me,
in believing that it's the decision I am making, on the anvil of my own freewill.

THRONE WITHOUT JUST THORNS

Life's too short, that's true; time moves exponen-
tially fast,
a void pokes our hearts wearily, to just fill it up,
with anything.
Choices are not meant to be choicest, a siren sings
mellifluous;
the eidolon of uncertainty looms too, "what if even
this passes by?"
Thus, our will crumbles, letting in knowingly, hurt
purposeful.

Life ought not have double rainbows, every moment of perfection,
but is it too much to ask for, having a decent run of
the mill experience?
Out of the infinite possibilities, which essentially is
life, must we
embrace a stem of thorns, even when there is no
rose, not now nor ever?
It's true there are two sides of things, but a looping
misery has none other.

Though it's easier said than done, to wait that is; for
there is no line drawn,
on time running mad keen, to when will it be over

and for better not worse.
In our beating hearts, the chords of longing are
struck, more and more;
each opportunity seems promising. No matter how
monochromatic it is,
our prism of expectations amalgamated with delu-
sions and ignorance,
makes us see colours, double rainbows even, where
only darkness prevails.

So I'd bet my life, on hard decision and taking re-
sponsibility, integrity and faith;
love will shine, singular and bright; when it does,
we will know, for it will make
us smile, only to catch ourselves in the act and wondering why we did.
Life will come the way it will come, we can only
have a mind like water,
receiving, not reacting. So when the moment opportune, of good fortune, knocks,
we will open our arms; just like we close, to what
imparts nothing but hurt.

PERSONA

My resolve, to revolve and not evolve is a thorn,
nipping my lotus in the bud, makes me stay in the mud.
But too many wolves are circling my city, day and night,
waiting for my mask to slip, for my story to flip.

Tender, raw and overflowing with emotions, my naive heart;
has had many stumbles, while beating for someone else,
so now I am a camouflage, hiding my truth from them and me.
My pain has forged me an armour, of indifference systemic.

Lately I've come to know, my show has garnered a new audience,
that my lies have woven a fabric to cover a set of eyes, mine.
Looking back, I can recognise myself, but who's in this mirror?
It's like my deception has shrouded my own perception.

I want to live again, love again, fly and float aging on
my broken wings;
more importantly, I long to let someone let me go of
myself, unto them.
But too well aware I'm, this can't happen; for I'm not
who I used to be.
This mask I donned on to hide, has changed me, irre-
versibly.

I guess that's the price one pays, for holding back the
tears and
lamenting all alone and forlorn, terrified of revealing and thus
unravelling once again, what happens if she doesn't.

FROM ASHES TO FIRE

Failure is not just something to shrug off, and move on from,
it's just as important as success, as it gives meaning to it.
When the world falls apart, no hope remains in sight;
on the anvil of that time, a character is forged, indomitable.
It's better to have loved, they say and losing doesn't matter;
for it's the singular act of rising in love, makes one a Phoenix.

If all the words just rearrange, like magic and turn into a poem;
that is as breathtaking as the "immolations", it won't take a breath,
for it will not have a piece of poet's heart, shimmer of herself poured.
Growing pains are not pains, they are growth; a troubled time
is not troubled, it's us who make it so, otherwise it's just an experience.

To embrace bliss, and let go of misery; to carry on

the quest of love,
avoiding despair; to laugh and never have the eyes
well up, is like
a bird never learning to fly, for the fear of falling;
falling is flying in part.
And if victory exists in every aspect, just to satiate
one's whims;
if in the book of love, no pages are blank or torn,
evoking an ache;
life will be livid, like a cold fire, piercingly unbear-
able, sans entice.

Life's destinations are just fragments of the journeys
we take and don't.
As I rise in her love again, when I am sitting alone
under the setting
autumn moon, knowing she exists only as a figment
of her physical;
and when I sing a serenade, recalling her name, skip-
ping a string.

FALTERING PRETENSIONS

Resembling the haughty frown on the face of the most mighty pharaoh,
barely surviving in grains of sand, illegible, far away from being indelible;
and cast away on the well trodden path, failing every hallowed promise,
my lonely self stares back at me, in hopes of realigning with what's lost.
But I'm gone, lost unto me.

In a skipped heartbeat, ego inflated to enormity, much to my chagrin;
not that I steered my thin veneer on the edge of losing it all though.
I knew within half a blink of your half moist lids, that it was over,
at once and for all but me, yet I clawed forth, persecuting myself.
Until I lost you, knowingly.

Days of summer were long and winding, at every crossroads you were;
nights of winter felt the ambers of your touch, making my heart waft
and every rain descended to meet your silhouette,

casted from behind
the moreen curtains, where your eyes shone, like
pearls in a sea of rain.
Such were my seasons, my reason.

Now that the self sabotage has attained florid fruition
and my life's but a limbo, an ever enlarging shadow;
I dream of a past, of a certainty not realised and
purposefully thrown away; knowing well, my love
to claim is but a few steps and strings of words away.

DARWINIANA

Mining for thoughts, finding treasures hidden by themselves,
The blind watchmakers are lost in search of facts of time.
Edenic verses sung at the top of their lungs, some, while
Others chop Noah's ark away, axing questions of Popper.
Churches all too divvied up.

Rolling their eyes they scoff and derogatory smirks spread,
On the faces of critiques of the creation of Adam.
Reconcile not, some say do, is it a theory or a fact?
Inept humans with anti-monkey laws, drowned still,
In the flood universal.

Conjecture runs amok, just covers of books change;
Underneath it all there is warping of language, open ended.
No one knows it all, it's like a game of chess where
A knight single handedly turns the laws upside down.
And until you know this rule, there is no way to

know it.

It's hard to imagine another dimension, like Ab-
bott's people,
For us too and to me just for that matter, its inconse-
quential
To ponder over known facts or dogmas with any
certainty.
Everything can be topsy-turvy, with one more
piece of the jigsaw,
Fitting differently but all too well.

FROZEN REFLECTIONS

Dusk setting on walls of the purgatory
between the promise of a good world
and crimes committed in a lapse,
some with premeditation, hell.
Sunshine less dazzling, as if through
frosted glass, reluctantly contours his face.
He ploughed the fields of blood,
first for bread and then couldn't stop,
to dread, or rethink, will his be undone.
It's wasn't revenge, nor righteous anger
but a momentum; set in motion by greed
of no ends and means to meet.
On a late stretching afternoon
blending into orange evening,
I asked him who he feared the most.
Was it the old judge,
who couldn't right his wrongs?
For all his fury and infinite wisdom,
the one before the son of god
can't make right, that which a man
did suffer from another.
My fellow pilgrim by force,
not compulsion, said it was not so.
And on a damp morning in muddied halls,
I asked him about returning to

DR. BHRATRI BHUSHAN

a hill of my dreams, where he will be
all taken care of, even if the ones
he wronged couldn't be raised till
the day of judgement. To which he
looked at me with eyes, piercing something
vague within my heart and shook his head.
When the dusk, thus is setting on the walls,
tomorrow gallops with a scythe
for bringing his night. In his silent mourning,
his realisation is sinking deep within
the quicksand of his scarred heart;
when he tells me, he wishes to die
and it the act, be lost, for all there is
but first to himself.

THE TRUTH

One signpost inviting to come back home,
Another a telltale of a home where the heart is.
This crossroads of life with a fine tooth-comb
Finds the hunter in me to the dismay of Venus.
My intentions were all fine back in the day
This life was a lyric of someone else's song;
I wish to act to if not uplift then tread too nay,
On dreams, hopes of my fellow men's spring.
In my life's ontology the Golden rule rendered
Tarnished though with malice brushed on palms
Of my hands, pushing to amorality inadvertent.
If I were to make a universal law of my psalms;
I would take what is equal not just, if I must,
For my decisions have been anything but.

Inscribed on layers of my conation is the notion:
What I think is the only truth, I'm the compass.
In my journey of finding, to what I'm in oblivion,
The needle points its whims that come to pass.
My actions need a license but surely not my own,
Though doctrines are just as flimsy, not normative.
Thus now I am on a quest like Gilgamesh, alone,
To find universality to reign over me and give
My life a meaning long overdue and restrain
Apostatizing to a faith of my own, my bane.

It comes to me at moments of reflections keen,
Should my reason be my custom or be arcane?
Answers beget more questions as I wade
Murky sky looming over fields of truth bade.

THROUGH AND FRO

1.
Determined to find the ocean,
a fish left her home of a coral reef.
At times it swam near the surface,
seeing the sun reaffirmed herself
that if it could find the sun,
how hard can it be to find the ocean.

It dipped below, when seagulls
squawked over and fought large
metal giants, sent by the ocean god,
like Quixote's windmills.
Night downed soon,
iridescent scales of other fish
in light of a bluish looking moon,
reflected to her, their ignorance
and spirit feeble; unlike her,
it mused.

Near the crack of dawn,
its fins began feeling heavy and
in dreams it drifted, half asleep
of finally finding this ocean
everyone talks about, this myth.
When it woke up, an old octopus

was floating by.
She thought it was wise to ask
for directions from an old one.
He told it to just open its mouth
and taste the ocean and went by.

2.
"Where has the tick gone, father?"
A boy asked, looking at a
disassembled clock.
His innocent mind wondered,
was the tick in the second hand
or may be in the spring coil?
His father assembled it again and
the tick came back, tick-tock.

His father then told him,
the tick is the soul,
comes on its own when
everything's right.

3.
The king was furious.
He was on a journey and
has been praying,
in the middle of a desert when
a girl ran knocking him over
in the middle of it.

He finished his prayers, smouldering
of anger and ordered his soldiers

to bring her to him.
And when they did,
he asked, "before I execute you,
for dishonouring me and that
too in the middle of a prayer,
do you have anything to say?"

The girl replied,
"Don't lie, my king, you haven't been
praying, I was. I was running
to meet my lover, he was waiting;
and I couldn't see, a king with his army.
Then how did you see me,
if you were praying to the king of all kings,
and lover of all lovers?"

DREAM LIKE AN EGYPTIAN

Kissing the sphinx, an illusion though a sight for eyes sore;
Your face resplendent, the vernal equinox of birth of dreams,
Making the Orion belt fade away, while your smile makes
Me long for memories once etched, a tide washed ashore.

Spreading arms against the ruins of yesterdays, glorified
By virtue of their existence and casting a shadow just as
Beautiful as the dance we had in the desert that moonless
Night, when rain descended rinsing us of our past.

In your aquamarine contacts, I see Nile spread as milky way,
Traversing through space and time as does a swift turn
Of your eyes towards me, validating and reassuring at once.
A boat undulating carries us towards a future tempestuous.

Walking in the streets of the city of mighty phar-
aohs fallen,
To Mit Rahina, the old capital, almost forgotten but
lively;
You hold my hand, your fragrance inebriating my
essence.
Timelessness gets hold of me, in a glimpse of your
face.

In this corridor of time, leading to the promise of a
life
Tad different than dreams but ever so surreal in aspect,
Past hangs around like a tapestry, while future still
Being knit, already foretold, only if it can survive
the tide.

EYE OF THE STORM, MY HOME

I saw orange sun peeking
Through a veil of morning mist;
A flock of birds spread like dots,
Changing directions abruptly
Like a silken curtain in the wind.
It had rained last night.

Climbing the rungs of time,
Sunlight golden stretched its embrace
As a thousand tantalizing glimpses
Of its reflection appeared in
The puddles, shallow and deep.
Changing with every step I took.

I could see my home,
Still covered in a blanket of fog,
Light seeping out of the windows
And a wafting fragrance which
Always lingers around, of jasmine
And tea roses blossoming.

A traveler goes around
The world to find in his home,
What he's been looking for.
I too, in my soul searching

Have stumbled upon the fact
That my home is my heart.

FAKE IT TILL YOU MAKE IT

It's me who is lost, and you've never known me.
Barging through my boundaries, the world comes,
Judging every move I make, every one of which a fakery.
Dolos walks with me, in every sway of my body;
In every smile rehearsed for those made up occasions
And flowers thrown backwards with gleeful smiles
Not one at a time, but as instructed, not too many as well.

It's you who I don't know, for you must never show
Your idiosyncrasies, unless an expert gives you a green light.
Jaw line should be more defined, even if it's a few
Masterful strokes of a scalpel away and oh, don't forget,
You must not forget, the fish lips and nose jobs and
The accidental crooked smile, you hate but can't live without.
Take your time to breathe in the fragrance of no consequence.

It's the world you must appease, by making yourself a travesty

So the void may be filled with passing remarks of complete strangers.

Pass-remarkable eyes will pierce your armour, quite literal, at times;

Vicious and almost flesh eating, visceral they say, but that's fine,

There is no such thing as bad publicity, so buckle up with Botox.

Relationships are a big cash cow, long as spicy gossip they endow

And break up like you put on makeup, expendable and all made up.

The rules are simple of this world within a world, first pretend it's real

Then forget you are real, reinvent yourself into a stale stereotype,

Devoid of even an iota of authenticity and whatever facade

You manage to pull together, should define you until they want it no more.

REASONABLE BEING

Soaring high or at times barely rising from the sur-
face
Of this ocean of awareness as a wave, destined to be
One again with the source, just a matter of time.
Yet for the time, I break free, I bask in a patch of
Sunlight of my own; am caressed by winds unlike
any
And could feel and fill a sky that belongs only to me.

I came in this world raw, as everyone else, a possibility
Of infinite potential manifestations, visceral and
heartfelt.
Before I even knew what knowing means, a machin-
ery,
Rather an assembly line, got hold of me and pack-
aged me
As it saw fit; indelible marks strained, irreversible
moulding,
Made me a cog of the juggernaut of collective delusion.

It's me, I say to you, living a lie and helping you to
live yours.
Numbness tarnishing perspective, to feel alive I

often shout
And declare who I am, seeking validation from the echoes.
I know it's all make believe, or at least never felt by heart once;
But how can so many old books be wrong, how can I be wrong?
If all this time I've been running in circles, then the circle must be
Getting somewhere, may be after a thousand and one revolutions
I may see a door opening; anyways it's too late to stop now.

I either go with the flow, existing but not being me or I adjust my sail
To battle the currents head on, a war cry and a blind rebellion.
If everyone's going west, I may head east, into a different kind of
Madness; but at all cost I avoid seeking myself where I know for a
Fact that I'll be: within me. For I know, if I align with my centre of being,
The thin veil of deception will not hold, the world will end as I know it.

I trust myself with my heart, it beats on its own.
I never think of breathing, it happens on its own.
Everything that matters, just happens; love, birth, death.

But I can't trust the universe for me being me,
I must take those reigns and gallop towards
Being someone who's not me, living a life
That's anything but alive and mine.

WHEN LEAVES ARE FLOWERS

In this mellower time of the year, a kaleidoscope
That brightens leaves with colors riotous, flowers
fading;
I rejoice this year's harvest, my life, as icy jaws inch
closer.
A hush before winter, a fresh breath of Indian Sum-
mer;
Warmth of a promise kept, close to my heart and
keen.
As a chill November wind scatters the morning
mist,
Sunrays descend in a hurry, nuzzling me with zest.
Future is on thin ice, past is etched in stone but this
Day as clear as sparkling wine, makes my heart soar.

ZENFLOWER

Dancing in the sun was too much work,
So now I just watch the sun dance.
A subtle change of vantage point and
Shift of perspective away, freedom awaited.

Worked a lot, even more than honeybees,
Never got any credit though, as everybody
Thought that I just danced and made faces.
Now I hide my sun drunk eyes behind shades.

Kites aren't high as me, I've made the sun
My sidekick; it does what it does and puts
Itself out when it's time for me to sleep.
It wakes me up too, quite obedient it's grown.

I see my neighbors wilt and fall off every day,
But that's not happening to me, for I don't
Think of death, nor of life, or of work and rest.
I just am, and when I'm no longer, the world
Won't be either and surely won't be the sun,
For why it would rise, but most importantly
There'll be no more haters, for whom I just dance.

WALLING DOORS

I am going through the wall,
not through the door.
Standing on a table,
in the middle of the ocean
to look at the shore.
Parting gifts I'm receiving
when I first land
and a few warm hugs later
I am resting to get tanned.

Before sunrise I am ready
for the evening.
I am standing tall
knee deep in mud and
toasting to my long life
with the firing squad
saying, "ready!"
I am not working hard
but I'm bleeding sweat dearly.

In the bubble far away from
Hubble, underneath insurmountable rubble
I hide. Though my snoring
while I daydream tells the thralls
where I'm and I whistle softly

with a smug smile as they draw closer.
Because I know that
I can go through the wall
and they will come through the door.

FIRMAMENT FROZEN

Teasing the strings of moonlight,
my only star in the night sky fades
with each passing day, going away.
A song is stuck in my head, in reverse;
in it love ends in the end and begins in the middle,
while I keep wondering about how I missed
the telltale signs of the end of us.

One afternoon of customary day drinking,
when I drifted in a dream of uneasy sleep,
sun was shining bright, illuminating
the window panes and bursting through
the frosted glass; then you appeared
and your touch felt surprisingly warm;
a convection of love embodied.
Your eyes took some time to appear
as beautiful, even more, than I remembered
and slowly I eased to the feeling,
like Novocaine shrouding my senses
and all I can recall now is warmth.
A sluicing rain splattered on the windows
and woke me up, to a sky overcast with greyish
gloom, bursting forth and utterly unwelcome.

I can take it in the stride of my forlorn heartbeats

that you no longer have the simplicity of a genuine
smile
nor the magic of a few words, as key notes of a symphony,
orchestrating the play of our lives and making me
feel,
what I always longed for and lived once, with you.
But it rents my heart asunder to see the lights dim
and colours of our double rainbow fading
in the black hole of time; and I can't live
with you not turning back, before you leave for the
day.

Words will not suffice,
nor will subtle, evanescent slips
to the memories of who we were.
In some moments of high clarity,
it all comes back to me but then
slips away, like I let myself slip,
through the cracks of my love for you.

NATURAM EXPELLAS FURCA

To say the words you want to hear,
to fall in line by proving a point without heart,
to declare my existence to stir a sense of obligation,
to hold on when it's way past the time to let go,
to lock horns with life when it gives what I don't want,
I live to repeat.

Nature comes back, forks, knives and cannonballs later;
the sudden urge to break free, of sinking right on the shore,
of amassing a fortune by selling everything I hold dear,
of slowly forgetting my crescendos of joys and being overly familiar with the nadir of the slow burn of success,
my life's a testament.

I need a miracle now, ashes pulled from thin air
or smiles remembered without contorted eyes;
may be in love for once and at once free too,
not blaming anyone for the tethering of emotions.

So give me hope if you can, or I'll find someone who

can't.
Come to the terms of love lessons learned and now enacted,
in a labyrinthine way that surely defies me, the one who drafted.
While I get ready for the crown of thorns, to my kingdom of status quo.

TIME AND AGAIN

A carpet of morning sunlight unfolds
through the window pearlescent with frost,
flocks of birds warming up for the day
and like the Indian Summer a part of me
is quivering out of existence, finally.

Wandering is fun, living like a Gypsy
in the realm of my mind's fabrication;
a saltatory, fidgeting chronic dissatisfaction,
is starting to evaporate though, like dew from
the petals of tea roses, delighted.

This feeling rising like the sun,
in my heart, of never leaving this place,
of living here till the end of my days
till the day of judgement and then some,
makes me love life more, intensely.

Another year has coursed through me,
days of fleeting glimpses rarely and
nights of feverish dreams, never registered.
Cycles of the sun are impregnating
the times with a nascent promise of another.

I wish upon the falling star, that I broke,

unhinged and then blamed for falling,
that life grants me acceptance this time.
Healing begins while the damage is yet
to be done and turmoil holds the horses.

Sun is crawling up now, still drunk from
the cold of the night before, heroically;
I feel a singularity dawning on me now
and a literal skip in my step, it's true;
as a promise kept, you walk towards me.

ME AND THE THREE GODDESSES

A flute transforms wind into melodies,
like time makes manifest connected dots
on the stretched canvas of entropy.
Colours are there in the soil, already,
so is the shape of a pot in clay lying idle;
and a journey too is born with a traveller.
Purpose is not different than intention.

A seed is already a tree, just needing
the brush of time to paint its leaves and stem.
Sometimes I wonder, of what am I a seed,
do I have it in me to absorb colours out of
seemingly nothing at all, a true alchemy?
Is my journey becoming a burden, do I need
to adjust my mast, throw away my compass?

In the desert of fiery days and freezing nights,
this life, with its many twists and turns circling
the themes of great excitements interspersed
among moments of numbing pain and eventual
indifference, I see a sundial lengthen, disappear.
Waiting for someone to happen, now or ever.
I let reason and expectations reign over me.

I sense a gravity of inaction, getting stronger,

with each risk not taken, each dice not rolled,
roadside flower not smelled, thought racket
not interrupted and a hand not held in comfort.
A part of me dies with every moment not lived,
and I comfort myself in gathering trinkets.
While life awaits, and rolls the golden carpet
of sun rays every morning for me and watching
me, intently, with her lunar cycles, of ebbs and
tides, making me live, one day to attain her fruition.

OLD HABITS, RENEWED

Measured cadences of lady luck,
An inveterate stand-off between roads yet to be
taken
And directions I know I'll never sally forth to
Are constantly drafting the landscape of my life.

A dream is born, in the glimmer of her tears
Still welling up and yet to cascade down in rivulets,
Making my heart sink, for I know I'll let her down.
I like to tell myself that its more like string-skip-
ping,
But I know it's already eaten through my chords.

It lies behind the shadows cast, my destiny,
Also powering the illuminated ball in the sky;
Yet how skilled I am in evasion of its infinite reach!

Blame is no more lately, not on me, nor projected;
Its more of an acquiescence now, pearly gates closed
awhile.
I run through this maze, navigating and breathing
hard,
Taking a beating at every step and vowing hard to
change.
Though she smiles, Fortuna, her veil no more hiding

What she has planned for me, may be its my destiny
After all.

SHADOWS OF CLOCK HANDS

I had all the time in the world.
Mornings were so well defined,
transitioning slowly into afternoons;
evenings were seemingly endless and
nights just flew by in a second.

Everyone around me was a possibility,
roads seemed less traversed,
each year was etched in memories,
dust stirred from passing footsteps
consolidated into stars and I was struck.

I had all the time in the world.
Passed on moments opportune,
didn't pick my hammer when the iron
of time was red hot and ready to be
moulded into a miracle of a lifetime.
Because, I thought, there might be
another moment, just as ripe if not more.

Looking back at the pages
of the book of my life,
that I turned hurriedly, without even
deigning to read a word,
they read nothing short of classics.

DR. BHRATRI BHUSHAN

And I want to go back to ink some more,
to burn less bridges if not build some,
to look deeply inside some souls
and to not be afraid of singing a song.
Not everything is a masterpiece,
nor everyone is more than a promise of being,
and I, for one, am far from being one to keep.

HARBINGER YOURS

This wind of late autumn
feels like it bears your touch,
it rustles the pale leaves and gives
their fallen grace a taste of sky again.

I can almost hear your whispers,
but your faint words are drowned
in the sound of your voice
and the sweet ache of my heart,
ruffled by memories of our evenings
begins to tell me stories that I wrote.

Looking up, I see the wandering star,
carrying a light reminiscent of your eyes;
and in the lengthening shadows
I feel you, being merged in mine, with me.
Stars begin to peek through the dark carpet
and the street of no name is filled
with your absence, my feet become heavy.

You know I would've waited,
long enough to worth your while;
A tear shed in perpetuity for the anticipation
of a barely perceptible smile.
But it was too much to ask,

like asking for this wind to stay,
and your essence to linger
just for a moment more.

A VESSEL OF LOVE

You came in the colored leaves of autumn,
I heard your footsteps in a melody by an artist I
knew not,
you looked at me through a sky tired of carrying an
ocean
and I felt as if I had discovered a new sense, a tran-
scendent one,
when one day I wanted to dance to the sound of
silence.

I know you are me and I you and so is everything
else,
hurtling through space and time, this form of your
love being played
knitting my fabric with the universe and just one
thread less.
The dancer and the dance are not two but one,
so is your manifestation of the world and in some
moments,
rare as they are common, a leap of faith occurs to
your arms.

When I looked at the endless possibilities, I saw
you,
aching to break free and yet calm because you're

already.

And that evening when I looked in your eyes, I knew, something was said without a word and it was our story.

Since the first moment, circular tides of times infinite,

you have been and so have I, been with you, being the world.

A SHORE AND MORE

By knowing that you are, I know
that I have indulged more than I should've;
an insatiable thirst takes over me and
so does a fulfilment, to suffice for a lifetime.

Sailing waters uncharted,
heeding at times to the Sirens of my due,
I have reached here, shores of your kingdom.
Lapping waves tell me that I can dock here,
in fact, it must have been my destiny
to find my temple in the midst of a tempest.

You must be here, somewhere,
or everything after meeting you is you,
as a whole, integrated and a gestalt?
A setting sun is lingering, with its webs of rays,
still spreading through the western horizon,
while it's already sunk at your feet
and a full moon is now taking shape,
to adore you, adorn you and guide me
to what I know will be my only truth.

A COUNSEL OF DESPAIR

Layers of mist
shrouding my world;
in the palpable warmth
of my own and in the faint
murmurs drowning my thoughts,
I move slowly, groping tentacles of time.

Dreams of doom,
nocturnal paroxysms;
wounds incurred, inflicted,
healing even more traumatic.
Sudden outbursts of strength by
all the wrong means; meanings too cryptic.

Why am I so insecure,
what are these dark waves
gnawing away the shores of my life?

Protecting my periphery,
a landscape of lies and make believe,
is a job endless, tiresome and a lost cause.

There'll always be
another threat, another matter
of life and death but never of life alone.

In all in this cacophony
is drowned my symphony of life
played constantly, since the beginning of time.

Even when it reaches me,
it falls on my ears so deaf and nerves so numb
that I mistake it for a song of another life, not my
own.

Such is my impasse,
I burn with a fever of losing
which was not worth having at all
and when I realise that the sands of my life
have reshaped the dunes of the desert of my existence,
and they do it time and again, I feel lost in an oblivion of my own.

www.ingramcontent.com/pod-product-compliance
Lightning Source LLC
Chambersburg PA
CBHW021508210526
45463CB00002B/941